ENGLISH FURNITURE

David Nickerson

OCTOPUS BOOKS

Acknowledgments

The author and publishers are indebted to Mallet and Son (Antiques) Ltd of New Bond Street, London, for supplying the majority of the illustrations in this book. They also wish to thank the following owners of pieces illustrated for permission to reproduce them: the Victoria and Albert Museum, figures 12, 38, 39, 40, 41, 42, 45, 50, 55, 81 and 129; the Mellon Collection, figure 4; K. Mason Esq, figure 6; Lt. Col. Keith, figure 13; the Bristol Art Museum, figure 14; Samuel Bronston Esq, figures 16 and 119; the Earl of Faversham, figure 29; Lady Vansittart, figure 47; P. Hopkins Esq, figure 58; Frank Partridge & Sons, figure 56; Claude Leigh Esq, figures 70 and 73, the Duke of Northumberland, figures 72 and 74; the Marinotti Collection, figure 82; Gerald Hochschield Esq, figure 86; Mrs W. Dunnington, figure 114; G. H. Garratt Esq, figure 127; F. L. Egerton Esq, figure 125; the Earl of Pembroke, figure 34; the Duke of Bedford, figure 37; the Soane Museum, figures 76 and 77.

The photographs of the following illustrations were taken by: E. & D. Gibbs, figures 1, 7, 11, 18, 20, 23, 24, 25, 26, 33, 44, 46, 53, 54, 57, 59, 60, 68, 92, 100, 108, 112, 126, 132; Messrs A. C. Coopers, figures 38, 39, 40, 41, 42, 45, 50, 55, 81; Edwin Smith, figures 34, 72, 74; R. B. Fleming & Co, figures 76, 77; figures 37 and 91 were supplied by the Radio Times Hulton Picture Library; the end-papers were supplied by the Walker Art Gallery, Liverpool.

Preceding page
A rare Chippendale black lacquer commode with a moulded border to the rectangular top, fitted with a long drawer to the frieze and with reeded tapering legs.

This edition first published 1973 by
OCTOPUS BOOKS LIMITED
59 Grosvenor Street, London W 1
ISBN 0 7064 0053 4
© 1963 by David Nickerson
Produced by Mandarin Publishers Limited
77a Marble Road, North Point, Hong Kong
and printed in Hong Kong

Contents

1 A William and Mary
marquetry secretaire cabinet on
a stand, about 1695.

4

UNTIL THE MIDDLE of the reign of Charles II, makers of furniture had relied on carving or panelling for decorative effect, but about 1670 a new style was introduced, mainly from Holland, of veneered work. This allowed plain surfaces to be inlaid with marquetry of the richest description, including ivory, ebony and other coloured woods, in the form of floral designs, birds or arabesques. This was especially effective on the fronts of cabinets, the tops of tables, longcase clocks, and on the drawer fronts and tops of chests-of-drawers. In the later work the

2 A Queen Anne walnut bachelor's chest, with a fold-over top.

3 An early eighteenth-century walnut library chair, with compartments in the arms and a drawer in the seat, sometimes called a 'cock-fighting' chair.

greater part of the design was worked out in two-coloured woods. On some pieces the pattern is dark and the ground light, whilst to give a richer effect the reverse was also done. In France André Boulle and his contemporaries produced much the same type of furniture using brass and tortoiseshell instead of veneers.

English furniture made at the end of the seventeenth and at the very beginning of the eighteenth century was greatly influenced by Dutch and French design, and by the arrival of Dutch cabinet-makers in the wake of William III. Among them was Daniel Marot, a French Protestant, who after working in Holland came to England and laid out the gardens at Hampton Court Palace. He was a draughtsman of ability and his designs introduced the English cabinet-maker to the French baroque style which flourished at the time. In its turn this style influenced designers like William Kent.

This new style was particularly noticeable in the design of chairs and contained several features which were developed later. Chairs hitherto had had very tall backs, containing a panel of cane-work between turned and carved supports; the wood used was either walnut, oak or some fruit-wood. The stretchers and friezes were elaborately carved with scrolls, while the legs might have a 'Spanish' scroll toe or twisted supports. The chairs were often decorated with gold or silver or red lacquer, and the backs and seats were covered in silk velvet to add to the appearance of grandeur in which people of the period delighted. Now the line of the chairs became simpler, and although the centre splat was often carved, this was the only carving, except for perhaps a scroll on the knee or at the toe. The chairs became

4 A pair of Queen Anne walnut chairs on cabriole legs and with splatted backs, about 1710.

5 A Queen Anne walnut side-chair, with a coat-of-arms carved in the seat rail. It is covered in its original needlework.

smaller and narrower, the stretchers were simple and for the first time the cabriole leg was introduced. This shape was prevalent for forty years.

Chair-making, which had previously required four separate crafts for the completion of a frame – the joiner, the turner, the carver and the upholsterer – now became a specialized craft, and remained so until the end of the century, for Thomas Sheraton in his *Cabinet Dictionary* says, 'Chair-making is a branch generally confined to itself'. During the reign of Queen Anne the high back became almost completely extinct, except for hall chairs which had solid, decorated backs and occasionally the coat-of-arms of the family painted on the back. The legs were usually cabriole, ending in either a club foot, a hoof foot or a spade foot, and stretchers were discarded during the reign of George I for they interrupted the line of the curves of legs. The backs were carved to match the design of legs and also to fit the shape of the user more comfortably. The seats were covered either in needlework or velvet and for the first time 'drop-in' seats were used. This meant that the chair-rail could be veneered, which added to the simplicity of the chair. The chairs became lower and a vase-shaped splat was used; in the beginning, this was inlaid with marquetry and later was veneered with carefully chosen walnut, the figuring of which added to the beauty of the chair. Winged chairs were made with short cabriole legs and a caned shell on the knee, for decoration.

As with chairs, so with settees; the taste changed during the reign of Queen Anne from the high-backed and elaborately carved to the low-backed and the simple. Instead of high padded backs shaped like two chairs and squat cushions, they became

6 A Queen Anne walnut love-seat, on cabriole legs, covered in contemporary needlework.

7 A rare George I walnut circular stool on carved cabriole legs, with claw and ball feet.

9 An early eighteenth-century black-lacquer bureau with gilt decorations.

8 A Queen Anne gesso torchère.

10 A William and Mary walnut card-table.

11 A mahogany and gilt torchère, of about 1725.

12 An early eighteenth-century black-lacquer hall-chair, with seat and back decorated with a coat-of-arms. It stands on shaped legs with gilt enrichments.

padded and covered in needlework, with perhaps a border of walnut which would contain the drop-in back. An alternative to this design was the settee with the double-spoon-backed splats, which had graceful 'shepherd crook' arms and stood on cabriole legs with claw and ball or pad feet. Settees were small, probably not more than four feet long, and have since been termed 'love-seats'. Day-beds were made, but not in large quantity and usually for the very rich. Stools with upholstered

13 A Queen Anne red-lacquer bureau-bookcase of about 1710.

seats were made in large numbers and were usually in walnut, or, if they were to be painted, beechwood. They were made in all shapes and sizes, but the circular and the oval stools are rarer than the rectangular ones. Stretchers changed from the shaped cross stretcher with a finial at the centre, in William and Mary's reign, to plain turned ones joining all four legs, at the time of Queen Anne, and subsequently disappeared altogether.

Beds at the beginning of the reign of William III were covered in material, usually velvet or silk. With the size and height of the rooms of the period increasing, the beds became immensely tall and were still curtained all the way round. However, during the

14 A walnut bureau-bookcase, with mirror doors enclosing many drawers.

reign 'half-tester' bedsteads began to be made and these achieved considerable popularity. In the bedroom, the chairs, settees and stools were often covered in the same material as the bed, and these materials were expensive. James II was supplied with 'Two Elbow Chairs, Six Stools, the Frames Carved and Gilt, all Suteable to the Bedde', by Simon de Lobell, a Parisian upholsterer. The bill was £1515, including, of course, the bed. During the first twenty years of the eighteenth century, the middleman in English industry gave active encouragement to the discovery of new methods of producing goods, and in this the clothier was no exception. In the textile trades there was always a shortage of yarn, for it was all hand-made and there was an ever increasing demand. Jealous of her own industries, England viewed those of other nations with envy. She had welcomed men like Marot before, and when the Loube brothers in 1716 managed to steal details of an Italian piece of machinery which made silk and had it patented, they were gratefully acclaimed.

Gold was becoming increasingly used for the decoration of the more important pieces of furniture, particularly mirrors, and men like John Pelletier, John Gumley and James Moore supplied William III, Queen Anne and George I with torchères, mirrors and tables. These were decorated with gesso. This was plaster, which was then 'cut in the white', and gold leaf was applied

15 A George II gilt-wood side-table with a marble top, and the legs carved with the heads of *putti*. The centre cartouche contains scrolls and bearded heads, in the style of William Kent.

16 An early eighteenth-century red-lacquer blanket chest, decorated with trees, houses and boats in gilt.

to a thin layer size. Looking-glasses were becoming increasingly used as decoration especially between windows where they were hung over pier- or side-tables. Glass was becoming cheaper, but it was still expensive, and its manufacture could be a matter of litigation, as when the Bear Garden House attempted to prevent John Gumley from continuing his glass manufacture. However, legislation preventing the closure of new glass-houses was passed in 1707. Bevelled glass borders were also used inside a narrow

17 A rare walnut bureau-bookcase with gilt finials and shaped top. The doors have gilt column supports.

gilt or silvered frame and *verre églomise* borders were also applied. This method of decoration by which colours, usually blue, red or green, had a design in gold imposed on them and were then applied to the back of the glass, originated in France, but was doubtless carried on in England. During Queen Anne's reign the cresting began to be made more solidly and was less pierced and had fewer scrolls. There was often a central cartouche with a coat-of-arms or a shell as ornament and the apron was carved in the gesso with floral designs. Brackets with grotesque masks and wall-sconces in gesso were also made. The tables, some for the centre of the room and therefore decorated on all sides, and others for placing against the wall, had tops most intricately carved with scrolls and with a centre medallion, or coat-of-arms

Another favourite form of decoration was lacquer in many colours, amongst them black, red, green, blue and cream. Pieces of lacquer had, at Queen Anne's accession, been imported for over a hundred years, but it was not until the Restoration that it became greatly popular. By the end of Charles II's reign the 'Coromandel Lacquer' which was known as 'Bantam work', because the Dutch had a trading station there, had become less fashionable than the lacquer with more gilt decoration and not incised. However, there are in existence commodes and chests of drawers made in the 1760's from Coromandel screens. At first, mostly screens, cabinets or pieces of lacquer were imported, cut up and applied to a piece of furniture; then attempts were made to copy Chinese designs into a surface of coloured varnish which was then polished and the design built up with paste and sawdust. The final decoration was made in gilt on the raised work and the unraised parts were drawn gently onto the ground-work. Leisured people looked on 'japanning' as a fashionable pastime after Stalker and Parker had produced a treatise on the art in 1688. The Europeans found that the Eastern cabinet-work was far inferior to their own and so furniture was sent out to the East to be decorated. There was not nearly enough of this furniture to meet the demand and the European lacquer provided most of the market. Even wall-panels and in some cases whole rooms were decorated like this. There is no difficulty in deciding between lacquer produced in Europe and that produced in the East, for the latter retains a far higher finish, is naturally far more finely drawn and even the mounts of the cabinets are of higher quality.

Despite the use of gold and lacquer, most of the furniture made during Queen Anne's and George I's reign was of walnut veneer. The woods most frequently used for the carcase of a piece of furniture were oak, pine and beech. Great care was taken to see that these veneers were placed so as to acquire most advantage from their figure and colour. When the lacquer panels of wood had been placed in the deal carcase, they were then banded with a narrow strip of wood usually placed on the cross, but feather

18 An early eighteenth-century mahogany bachelor's chest with a fold-over top and its original handles.

20 A walnut bachelor's chest of about 1710.

19 A fine gesso upright mirror, with carved cartouches and borders. About 1720.

banding was also much used. Mouldings were used too, to enrich the plainer pieces; these were added to drawer surrounds and were usually oval-shaped, thus slightly sinking the drawers into the front of the cabinet or chest. These mouldings could be applied to the tops and bottoms of pieces as well. Foreign cabinet-makers of the type of Marot or Gerreit Jensen introduced finer methods of construction, and these were constantly improved on. Dovetailing provides a good example of this. Prior to about 1690, dovetails were made which went right through and so each pair and dovetail was open on fine surfaces. This made veneering difficult and so a 'lapped' dovetail was produced. The dovetails became smaller as techniques improved. When looking at a piece of walnut furniture of fine quality, one also notices that the sides of the drawers are made with a runner at each side and there is a groove cut to fit these runners exactly in the side of the carcase: however, on a piece of less fine quality a piece of wood is merely nailed to the bottom of the drawer.

Many new designs for pieces of furniture were produced in the late seventeenth century and early eighteenth century. Card-tables which folded so that they might be placed against the wall were made either of half-round or rectangular shapes. Some had the tops covered in needlework with playing cards, or people playing at cards worked in the finest petit-point. They also had cups in walnut sunk into the top to hold money. Narrow book-cases had glazed doors and plain astragal bars similar to the ones

15

21 A fine Queen Anne gilt and gesso table. The top is decorated with arabesques and a centre panel with a coat-of-arms.

made for Samuel Pepys. Many writing pieces, some with fall-fronts known as 'beuros', some with fall-fronts known as 'scrutoirs', were designed for use in bedrooms as well as living-rooms. Bureau-bookcases were also introduced, usually of the finest quality. The tops of these pieces were either double domed, which was the earlier form, or straight. The doors were often mirrored and enclosed either shelves or numerous small drawers and pigeon-holes. The fall also hid more drawers and a well which often contained secret drawers or compartments. Below the fall are four or five drawers divided with two small ones at the top and probably three long ones below. Narrow chests-of-drawers, now known as 'bachelor chests' also appeared, with a fold-over top to write on or to act as a dressing-table. The tall-boy and the chest-on-stand were first made and even some of these pieces, used above all for the keeping of clothes, had writing drawers fitted in them.

22 A pair of walnut armchairs, the seats and back covered in floral needlework, and the front legs cabrioled with carved ball and claw feet.

The furniture of Queen Anne's reign was restrained in its ornamentation and admirable in its proportion. These characteristics were continued into the reign of George I. The embargo placed by the French in 1720 on the walnut wood forced English cabinet-makers to look elsewhere for their supply of wood and they started to bring in walnut from Virginia which was of a much tighter grain and darker in colour. They also started to import mahogany. This wood was found to be more useful than walnut in various ways. It was very durable, it was not attacked by worm, it acquired a very good polish easily and it could be made a good, rich-red colour which much appealed to the taste of the time. It could not however be made easily into veneers. Probably its greatest merit was that it was admirable for carving, and so in place of well-chosen veneers, applied enrichments were added. Another important virtuc of mahogany was the size of the tree, which was especially useful in the making of dining tables.

23 A mahogany wine-cooler of about 1730.

25 A pair of walnut and gilt wall-lamps, dated 1725.

24 A mahogany kettle-stand with a triangular fret top of about 1735.

26 *(opposite)* A mahogany bookcase with an architectural pediment and gilt enrichment. The doors and drawers are decorated with a Greek key-pattern.

The old form of gate-legged tables was modified slightly by supporting it with cabriole legs, and club or claw and ball feet. Also the first type of extending table was devised, which consisted in a pair of tables with square flap tops which were added to the centre pieces when required, and being used as side-tables when not otherwise needed. This led naturally to the production of an extending table with extra leaves.

The introduction of machogany did not greatly alter taste during the early years of George II's reign. Chairs, settees and tables of similar design could be purchased in either walnut or mahogany. Carving of great quality is shown in some of the seat furniture of the period, and was almost exclusive to the apron on the seat-rail and to the front legs. But an eagle's head or a lion's head might be used for the end of the arm. The knee of the leg was most boldly and deeply carved with lion, or human masks, or satyr or Indian heads. The foot ended in a claw and ball, a scroll or a paw with deeply carved hair. These designs were much copied during the time when furniture of this age was most popular and plain examples had features carved out of the existing wood. These can usually be distinguished by the shallowness and lack of sharpness in the carving. What made deception easier was that there were no set forms, and rare pieces could be produced and passed off as period furniture. The chair-backed settee also continued to be popular and was extended so that it might have three chair backs in the frame. These were made as sets with perhaps twelve single or armchairs and four stools as well as the settees. Tall-boys were also made and had slight alterations made to them; they might have a canted corner which was sometimes enriched with a carved motif or they might be standing on carved feet; and very rarely they have a secret drawer concealed between the two top drawers. Ladies used small dressing tables on cabriole legs and with three drawers in

18

the frieze or a small kneehole table which had a cupboard in the centre surrounded by drawers. These occasionally had a fitted drawer, but more often the looking-glass stood on top.

An invention of the period was the tripod table which stood on cabriole legs with claw and ball feet and had either a plain or most finely carved stem. The top could have either a plain or a shaped edge, the latter being often in the same form as a silver salver. These tables were used for the drinking of tea and were placed in convenient places near chairs and sofas. Kettle-stands were also produced for the tearoom. It is important to remember that there was a considerable time-lapse between the adoption of a style by the court and its comprehension and use by the rural cabinet-maker. Also people tended to concentrate their finer and more up-to-date furniture in the living-rooms and take the old pieces from them to their bedrooms.

During the early 1720's Lord Burlington started to press for a return to the style of architecture followed by Palladio in Italy during the sixteenth century and also by Inigo Jones in England during the seventeenth century. He had met William Kent in Italy between 1712 and 1719, where they had as a travelling companion Thomas Coke who had inherited large Norfolk estates in 1707. Coke, on his return from the grand tour, when he acquired many fine pieces of sculpture and a great collection of works of art, commissioned Kent to build a suitable house in which to keep his treasures. They both were devoted to Italy and so it was from that country that the inspiration for the great house came. Lord Burlington, although not a great architect or designer himself, attracted to him many architects of great talent, among them Colin Campbell, who designed Houghton for Sir Robert Walpole, and Mereworth, which is almost a facsimile of Palladio's Rotunda, and Leoni who designed Moor Park for Benjamin Styles. At a time when patronage was all-important, Burlington was able to press the claims of his friends in the right quarters.

Kent was interested in furniture design, and as neither Vitruvius nor Palladio had written anything about the furnishing of their palaces or made any drawings for furniture, it remained for Kent to produce pieces in scale and keeping with his architecture. He therefore produced drawings for pieces which were meant to enhance the magnificent halls and saloons in which they were placed. Like Robert Adam later in the century, his chimney-pieces, his doorways, his windows and even his gardens were visualized as part of the whole concept of a house. If Campbell was the architect for Houghton, it was Kent who made the drawings for most of the furniture, and it is possible that Benjamin Goodiom made some of it. This furniture was made to stay in the house for which it was designed. In a letter written at Houghton to Frederick, Prince of Wales, Lord Hervey says, 'The

28 A William Kent wall-mirror with a gilt-wood surround and grotesque and feathered cartouches.

27 (opposite) A George I green-lacquer long-cased clock with panels of cream lacquer, by Edward Moore of Norwich.

furniture is to be green velvet and tapestry, Kent designs of chimneys, the marble gilded and modern ornaments.'

This type of furniture, of course, had no great influence upon the designs used for the general population. It was far too ornate and magnificent to be used anywhere but in a great house. The pieces consisted mainly of bookcases, mirrors, side-tables, pedestals and centre-tables. For the most part, the side-tables or centre-tables and pedestals were very richly carved and gilded. This was necessary to prevent the rooms appearing too cold. Kent used excellent craftsmen to create his newly designed

21

furniture and the pieces are remarkable for their fine execution. Many new forms were used, among them fabulous beasts, animals, cupid's heads, dolphins and eagles which took the place of the more usual supports for tables. The tops of these tables were often made of marble or scagliola brought from Italy, but some were also made in gesso. The most remarkable features were their size and the freedom of their design. A type of console-table which was to remain popular for some time was the eagle with the spread wings standing on a rocky pinnacle, the top of marble; this form continued to be made for a number of years because it could be used in smaller houses.

Despite the many new features, the furniture was still designed as far as possible on architectural lines, although not necessarily purely lines of Webb or Inigo Jones. The Palladians drew also from the example of the French designers of the end of the seventeenth century like Marot. This mixture of style is particularly noticeable in mirrors which have the simple outlines of the pediment, enriched from below by carving and scrolls. Torchères too changed greatly from the simple lines of the Queen Anne gesso stand [figure 8] to the more massive and grand ones of figure 29 with their caryatid heads and carved supports.

Although William Kent did not die until 1748, during the later part of the 1730's there were signs of a change of taste away from the architectural characteristics of the previous decades. Not that this was an immediate development, for in 1740 Batty and Thomas Langley produced a book called *A Treasury of Designs*, in which most of the drawings show a predominantly Palladian line. In 1744, John Vardy published a book titled *Some Designs of Mr Inigo Jones and Mr William Kent*. In this book, the Palladian influence is still strong but there are also indications that the author had studied the French Rococo style, which did not be-

29 One of a pair of finely carved pinewood terms by William Kent.

30 A fine pair of William Kent mahogany desks
with ormolu enrichment.

31 A Chippendale carved gilt-wood mirror with a Chinese decoration of phoenixes and C-scrolls.

32 A mahogany kneehole desk.

come truly popular until the 1750's; for it had taken over a century for England to form a background of classicism, and it was not lightly to be swept away. Indeed many of the patrons of the arts and other educated men remained true to the classical ideal throughout the century, and few architects attempted to master the French style which resulted in the Rococo ornamentation when it did appear, being very different in feeling from its counterpart across the English Channel.

In France the Rococo movement was a slow development and its origins may be traced back to Roman times. In it, continuous curves embraced the whole design and thus architectural features such as architraves were not used as decoration for furniture. The lengthened S and the C scroll became the dominant form. These two shapes became increasingly popular and during the 1750's were adapted to many pieces of furniture other than the chair leg which, with the adoption of the cabriole, was in advance of the times. Fronts and sides of commodes became bombé or serpentine shaped, creating overall shapeliness. With looking-glasses and wall-decorations, the lines remain thin and clean-cut, the carving precise and fine, acting only as a frame for the glass or picture. The English craftsman and designer generally failed to appreciate the nature of the style he was copying and it is not until Mathias Lock's books, *Six Sconces*

33 A pair of George II white and gold torchères.

34 A settee in the Double-Cube Room at Wilton
House, attributed to William Kent.

35 A superb George II bookcase veneered in
rosewood with an architectural pediment. The
doors are enriched with carved swags of corn and
flowers.

(1744) and *Six Tables* (1746) that we find an Englishman ably
handling the French Rococo style.

During the years from 1735 to 1750 the French taste gained in
popularity. More varied motifs were used for the making of
chairs and settees, but the shape of the chairs and settees themselves remained fairly constant. The frame of the seat which had
been shaped became square or serpentine, with a floral cartouche carved in the centre. The solid splat of the back, which
had shown the well-chosen veneers to such advantage, was
pierced and enclosed in a light rectangular frame, with a carved

36 A detail of the base of the bookcase shown in figure 35. It is surmounted by a key-pattern border and contains finely made drawers and cupboards.

and shaped back rail. The cabriole leg became finer and ended with a scroll over the foot, c. 1740, or a pad or claw and ball. The knee was often carved with C scrolls and leaves.

Upholstered settees were made and still covered in needlework and damasks, the legs were cabriole with claw and ball or paw feet and generally the development followed the design of the chairs. The upholstery was usually tight-covered and cushions in needlework were used.

Tea tables which stood on tripod legs had been produced first during the previous twenty years; they now had their supports elaborately carved and pierced, occasionally with columns arranged to form a box at the top of the pedestal. The tops were revolving, and being in mahogany, could be made very thin. This type of table led to the invention about 1730 of the dumb waiter – a table with two, three or even four tiers, which was placed beside the dining table so that people might help themselves from the decanter or plate that they required. Another type of tea table was rectangular in shape and stood on four legs. These have a pierced fret gallery round the top or the earlier ones have a top with 'rose and ribbon' border and no gallery. This form of decoration was also used for card-tables, but very plain rectangular-topped tables which fold in half are common. The cabriole leg was greatly used, but it had become more refined and had lost much of its strength; however it was considered indispensable to the French taste. Dressing tables continued to be very similar in design to the walnut ones of the first years of the century, made with a kneehole surrounded by small drawers and with one large drawer across the top. This drawer was sometimes made with compartments and a looking-glass which folded down.

An invention of the age was the commode 'chest-of-drawers' in the French style, a variation of which is illustrated [figure 20]. It was generally placed in the living room and was made of mahogany, serpentine shaped and standing on bracket or ogee feet. Unlike the French, these commodes were simple and unornamented except for occasional carving on the corners in the form of acanthus leaves or lions' heads with rings through their mouths. An exception is the very elaborate 'bureau chest', more French in style.

The interest in Chinese designs increased during the years from 1735 to 1750 and was to be a dominant style for the next ten years, probably as much because they were so diametrically opposed to Renaissance classicism as any other reason. There appeared to be no discipline about the decoration on Chinese furniture and porcelain, yet the results were perfect. This lack of apparent form led copyists to extraordinary fancies, far away from anything recognizably Chinese, and it gave them also freedom for their imaginations.

THOMAS CHIPPENDALE

THOMAS CHIPPENDALE was born in Yorkshire in 1718, the son of a joiner, and it is probable that, aged about twenty, he was apprenticed to a London firm of cabinet-makers for in 1753 he moved to a house in St Martin's Lane which was then an important thoroughfare. In addition, famous people, like Sir Joshua Reynolds, Francis Hayman and Sir James Thornhill, either had studios or lived in the street. Also living there was John Cobb who made the commode [figure 55] and was a partner of William Vile the cabinet-maker to George II and Queen Caroline. In 1754 he first published the *Gentleman and Cabinet Makers' Director* which was to make him famous.

Although books of furniture design had been published on the Continent as far back as the sixteenth century, these had usually been the works of architects who wanted to include drawings of furniture with those of their houses. In the earlier part of the eighteenth century too, this practice had been continued, but none until Chippendale appears to have produced a book ex-

37   The Chinese room at Woburn Abbey, containing Chippendale chairs in the Chinese style.

38 (opposite) A Chippendale lacquer bedstead with a pagoda-shaped top and lattice back.

clusively for furniture on the same scale. The book was dedicated to the Earl of Northumberland, and it is interesting to note that besides the names of the many wealthy people who subscribed to it, there are the names of many cabinet-makers, carvers, joiners and upholsterers. The book sold for £2.8.0 on the first edition and for £3 on the third edition, and consists of sixteen plates, which were engraved by Matthew Darly and by T. and J. Muller dated 1753 and 1754, in the first edition, and two hundred plates engraved by Darly and Muller with B. I. Taylor, J. Hulett, W. Foster, Herrerick and Maris in the third edition.

Chippendale must have been a man of considerable business acumen for he realized that a book of this kind would greatly add to his reputation and he recognized that the Rococo style could be used to his advantage. It is probable that Mathias Lock, the most skilled and enlightened of English draughtsmen in the French manner, was working for Chippendale during the 1750's and 1760's, for the collection of drawings by Lock in the Victoria and Albert Museum had drawings by another hand, possibly Chippendale's, amongst them. Lock produced books of designs before 1754, but published nothing further until 1769. A drawing by Lock for a mirror and console is illustrated [figure 45] and

39 A black-lacquer commode in the Chinese taste. Both the bedstead and the commode come from Badminton.

40 A drawing for a mirror by Chippendale, similar to that by Lock shown in figure 45.

may be compared to a drawing by Chippendale [figure 40].

At the time of the first publication of the *Director* the two styles most prevalent were the Chinese and the Gothic; the first had considerable influence both on the Continent and in England, but the second was almost exclusive to England. The two became interwoven and Chippendale uses them indiscriminately. Among the features most commonly used and borrowed from both sources was lattice work, which was applied to the backs of chairs, the doors of cabinets, the edges of tables and even the backs of beds [figure 38]. This lattice work was then used as a thin fret and was made to apply to the Gothic taste as well.

In the *Director* of 1754, there are thirty-eight new designs for chairs and there is not a single drawing of a chair with a claw and ball foot, and altogether little allowance is made to the past. Variations of the Chinese and Gothic taste are shown in fifteen of the drawings, indicating their popularity. The Chinese taste offered the greatest variation and was according to Chippendale 'most useful'. Types that most usually survive have plain latticed backs on square, either plain or pierced supports, with a corresponding stretcher. Few of the elaborate designs drawn were probably made in their exact detail and Chippendale draws all the front legs differently to give greater scope to the cabinet-makers. The Gothic designs have most exotically carved and shaped backs pierced or shaped with arches, and with the back rail topped with enrichments. The seat-rails have applied frets and are joined to the legs at the corners by pierced trellis or carved scrolls. The seats were often leathered and studded, a device of which Chippendale was especially fond.

Apart from the Chinese and the Gothic there are drawings for 'ribbon-backed' and 'French' chairs; three of the first are especially good, and of them Chippendale wrote that he had neither seen nor made any finer chairs. A chair of this type is in the Victoria and Albert Museum, London, and is a very fine example. Here the influence is mainly French with the cabriole leg having become finer and the chair-rail decorated. The motif of the back, with its C scrolls and interlocking ribbons is not new, originating on the Continent, and is especially typical of the Rococo period. Country makers made much use of these designs and greatly simplified them, using a straight leg and pierced splat and enriching them with much less elaborate carving. The ladder-backed chair was also made with straight cross-pieces to the back, like the treads of a ladder. These types of chairs found their way into many English houses. There are two designs for what Chippendale calls 'French' chairs which are similar to what have become known as 'Gainsborough' chairs. These are large and comfortable and as a rule upholstered. The backs were either covered in needlework or leather, but seldom had a carved border, being usually studded. The legs were

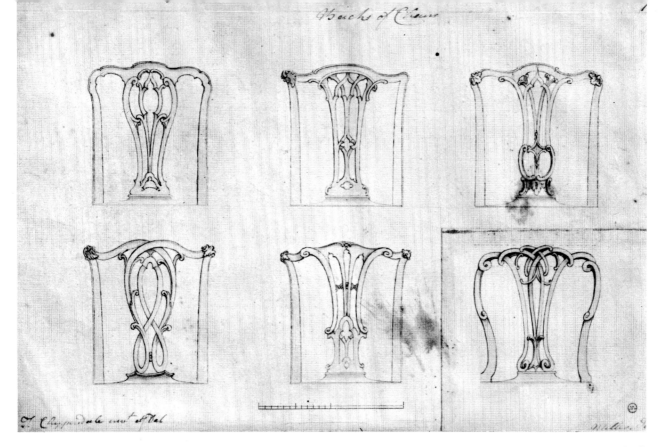

41 Six chair-backs included in Chippendale's *Director*, third edition, 1762.

42 'A visit from the solicitor'. A contemporary illustration showing mid-eighteenth-century furniture in use.

either cabrioled or in the Chinese or Gothic taste, with applied fret. They could also be just plain square, relying on the shape of the back to give elegance of line. Again simpler versions of these chairs were made in large numbers and sometimes in sets.

Furniture of imposing and important types like commodes, dressing-tables, bureau-bookcases, library tables and break-front-bookcases also appear in the *Director* and among Chippendale's other drawings. The commodes are of especial interest for they were to become pieces of great importance in the drawing-room. This piece had originated in France during the century and had influenced the making of chests-of-drawers in England during the previous decade. The pieces illustrated in the *Director* of 1762 show strong French influence although the material used was usually mahogany, which was not true in France. The commode relied on the richness of its carving and the boldness of its lines, rather than on ormolu and inlay, for its magnificence. Commodes of this period are rare and few can be ascribed to Chippendale with any degree of certainty. There was one at Raynham Hall in Norfolk and another at Chastleton in Oxfordshire, but in neither case has the bill from Chippendale survived.

Another design which appears for the first time and which shows similar influence to the commodes, is the dressing-table, which became more important than at earlier times. There is a drawing in the *Director* of 1762 for a piece surmounted by a

31

44 A Chippendale mahogany commode in finely figured wood with boldly carved panels.

mirror which is draped with material, and is boldly carved. The front has a recess in which there are drawers and is flanked by two sets of cabriole legs. There is also another which was described as a 'Dressing-table for a lady', made in rosewood with gilt enrichments. Two examples were shown which are much simpler and resemble a pedestal desk, but which have a closed kneehole with a cupboard. Like pieces of a decade earlier, these had a top drawer fitted with compartments and a mirror and only occasionally have any form of decoration. They were also much smaller in size, being only three feet, nine inches wide as opposed to five feet, two inches on the more elaborate tables.

There are many drawings for library-tables, bureau-bookcases and breakfront-bookcases and these again are often large and heavily carved. There is a very fine table at Nostell Priory for which Chippendale was paid £72.10.0. in 1767, and which is described as being 'of very fine wood' and 'finished in the most elegant taste'. For the table (Plate 58 in the *Director* of 1754), as for many other pieces, Chippendale supplied measurements and proportions, which he considered very important. The width is eight feet and the depth four feet and the height is divided most carefully for each moulding. This piece often had drawers

43 A mid-eighteenth-century mahogany bookcase with an architectural pediment and straight astragals and a pair of mahogany chairs.

45 A drawing by Lock for a mirror and console-table.

46 A mahogany tall-boy with a fret border, about 1745.

on one side and cupboards for keeping portfolios on the other, being designed to stand in the centre of the room. The usual motifs were used for the decoration of drawer-fronts and door-panels and the drawers were sometimes lettered.

Bookcases are given considerable prominence and here the Palladian influence still survives in the architectural pediment and severer drawing. The centre wood part has two doors and is supported by two wings which stand back, the corner is plain as are the glazing bars, which were removed completely when wire mesh was used for the doors; the base is also plain. On occasions

47 A pair of Chippendale japanned armchairs
with trellis backs and arms.

48 A pair of Chippendale carved mahogany
dining chairs with a pierced and carved splat.

49 A pair of mid-eighteenth-century mahogany
side chairs showing the Gothic influence.

secretarial drawers were put into the centre and the piece then had a double purpose. These bookcases were made to take the place of fitted shelves along at least one side of the library and so could often be very large. There are many variations as to the type of decoration and the pediment could have either a swan's neck shape, or broken arch, or a plain triangle. Marble busts were placed in the centre and on the ends and small pediments were occasionally made for them. The bookcase illustrated has straight glazing bars and cornice while the door panels have carved paterae [figure 53]. Gothic bookcases are illustrated in all three editions of the *Director*, but were seldom completed exactly as drawn.

The bureau-bookcase is also illustrated and had many variations on a theme. Their base or bureau has three long and two short drawers on plain or ogee bracket feet or again occasionally it stands on cabriole legs in which case the drawers are narrower.

50 A writing-table in mahogany with lion-mask decorations of about 1750-1755.

The top of the base has a fold-over front enclosing pigeon-holes and drawers, while the top has either glazed or solid doors enclosing shelves. The example illustrated has an unusual bombé base, and shaped drawers to the interior – the pediment is swan-necked with carved paterae and is pierced. The glazing doors are latticed, but this work has little relation either to true Chinese or true Gothic work [figure 52]. It is interesting to compare this piece with the illustration of the secretarial bookcase [figure 53], which has similar features but a very different rendering, the cornice as well as the pediment being pierced and the tracery being different in character.

The Chinese and the Gothic styles were both favoured for china cabinets and stands, and lacquered ones were made for the room at Badminton which contained the bed [figure 38]. As a rule these pieces were made in mahogany and consisted of a cabinet on a stand with shelves divided for the holding of china. The top was drawn to resemble a pagoda or had the cornice carved in the Gothic manner.

52 *(below left)* A mahogany bureau-bookcase with shaped astragals to the doors and an unusual *bombé* formed base.

53 *(below right)* A mid-eighteenth-century mahogany secretaire bookcase. The top has a pierced swan-neck pediment and the base contains drawers; about 1760.

54 A mahogany bureau-bookcase with a pierced swan-necked pediment, about 1755.

Side-tables and sideboard-tables were drawn in the first edition of the *Director* and vary from the most elaborate pierced designs to the most simple with scarcely any form of decoration. The former exists in both the Chinese and the Gothic – there being a fine example at Corsham Court. The latter is of course more often seen, for it went well with the chairs being made by the country cabinet-makers. These plain tables are found with marble tops, but the marble is usually plain rather than inlaid. Surprisingly, there is no design for a dining table in the Chippendale drawings, and it is not until nearer the end of the century that changes were made. The usual table was made up of two ends each with a half which could be raised and which stood when in use on a leg which swung forward. These legs were usually plain. There was an alternative which consisted of a centre section which remained permanently in place and to which two ends and extra leaves could be added. With so much concentration on chairs and side-tables it seems strange that so little interest was shown in producing an interesting drawing for a dining table. Another interesting addition was the breakfast or supper table, which was small and usually had either a single or two hinged flaps. The bottom was encased with either wire-mesh or lattice work and formed an open cupboard, presumably for keeping food. The very fine example [figure 87] has serpentined sides and one of the drawers is fitted with a slide for writing. The legs are inlaid and the oval panel is of figured mahogany.

There is a drawing in the Victoria and Albert Museum for a chandelier in carved wood, which came from the George Lock collection and was drawn about 1760. Not many chandeliers were made in carved wood, but there is one at St Giles House in Dorset, where Chippendale is supposed to have worked, and another of very similar design which came from Hornby Castle. These are both perhaps a little earlier than the one in the drawing.

Mirrors became increasingly important parts of the decoration of houses and the idea of placing them above console- or side-tables in halls and drawing-rooms continued. The style of these pieces changed abruptly and the plain Georgian mirror-frame with the architectural pediment was replaced by a form on which curves and S and C scrolls took their place. Designs were extremely diverse and ornamented with pagodas, Chinamen, phoenixes, animals, birds, pastoral scenes, icicles, leaf-work and flowers. This form of work was above all the province of the carver, and besides Chippendale, who shows many designs, Lock and Thomas Johnson also produced handbooks. Lock produced four more books in 1768 and 1769, with designs for sconces, torchères, tables, girandoles, pier-frames and even a separate book on the drawing of foliage 'for the Instruction of the Young Artists'. Thomas Johnson produced a book in 1755, which had a second edition in 1761, and another in 1760 of which nothing but a title leaf is known. Although he states that 'the designs may all be performed by a Master of his Art', many of the drawings are of amazing complexity. However there are a number of pieces by him, notably at Hagley Hall and Corsham Court which seem to substantiate what he says. There is also a stand in the Victoria and Albert Museum which has dolphins, a Chinaman, icicles and C scrolls, all most minutely carved. Another of his favourite devices seems to be the use of long straight columns, standing on either a rock or a small plinth, with the top of the column supporting a large scroll. He was also fond of the use of animals, and the carvings round his girandoles portray some of Aesop's fables. Another form of mirror which lent itself to the Rococo style was the overmantel which could be divided into sections at the sides, with a pagoda or some similar

55 An inlaid commode of *bombé* shape with ormolu enrichments, made by John Cobb.

56 A black-lacquer semi-elliptical commode with ormolu ram's head decoration of about 1770.

device dominating the centre part. Also small sections were carved which allowed for pieces of porcelain to be placed on them, adding to the richness of the effect.

It must not be supposed that Chippendale was the only great cabinet-maker of his day, for although the book of designs which he published was to make his name, and deservedly so, there were other men who were as fine craftsmen as himself, notably Ince and Mayhew, Vile and Cobb, and Robert Manwaring. Ince and Mayhew produced *The Universal System of Household Furniture* in 1759–63, and kept a shop in Soho. The book was dedicated to the Duke of Marlborough, and with the exception of a section on metalwork all the plates were designed by the proprietors. They also sent designs to the *Household Furniture in the Genteel Taste* for the year 1760 by a Society of Upholsterers

41

57 A Chippendale mahogany secretaire with a pierced fret compartment for books.

58 A very rare mid-eighteenth-century side chair with a show-wood frame and covered in its original needlework.

59 A fine Chippendale mahogany settee with scroll-carving decoration.

60 A mid-eighteenth-century mahogany desk with carved corners and shaped fronts.

61 A very rare mahogany desk for four partners of about 1760.

but although these drawings are recognizable, there are very few pieces of furniture which can definitely be ascribed to the firm. Vile and Cobb were the cabinet-makers to George III and Queen Caroline, and their work was of the highest quality and is renowned for its carving. There is a pair of cabinets for medals which are of the finest craftsmanship. The commode [figure 55] is attributed to Cobb and is in the collection of the Victoria and Albert Museum. Robert Manwaring is chiefly remembered for the publication of three books. In 1765, he issued the *Carpenters' Compleat Guide to the Whole System of Gothic Railing* and the *Cabinet and Chair-makers' Real Friend and Companion*. This was

62 A Chippendale mahogany standing cabinet with fret enrichments, about 1760.

reprinted in 1775. Most of the designs are reasonably practical and, as Robert Manwaring says, they could be made by a tolerable workman, and he had almost invariably made them himself. Many of the designs are rather rustic when compared to the work of Chippendale, but they were meant to be made from 'the Limbs of Yew, Apple or Pear trees' and then decorated.

During the years from the publication of the third edition of the *Director* until 1766 not a great deal is known of the work or life of Chippendale, but in that year his partner James Rannie died and the stock in trade was sold in St Martin's Lane. It was then that the accounts start for the furnishing of Nostell Priory and a year later for Mersham Hatch. In 1771 Thomas Haig was taken in partnership, but it is not known when his son joined the firm. In the same year the accounts start for the furnishing of Harewood House. The accounts which exist from the various houses mentioned above, and the accounts in the Victoria and Albert Museum of the work done for Garrick at Adelphi Terrace, are interesting from two points of view; first they describe in detail the work of Chippendale in the houses, the making of furniture and its cost, the mending and moving of it, the supplying of curtains and wall-hangings; and secondly, they show that although so few pieces survive, Chippendale must have been a man of considerable importance and well-known.

The first of these bills from Nostell Priory is of special interest, for it dates from the same year that Robert Adam designed the library, following James Payne. There are pieces of furniture, notably chairs, in the house which do not show any influence of Adam's and there are others which do reflect his style. The chairs cost £6 each, and while a plain desk cost £12, the finely carved one cost £72, but twelve rush bottom chairs could be had in 1766 for 2/6 each.

64 Three mid-eighteenth-century buckets. The one on the left was used for peat and the other two for coal.

65 A finely-carved Chippendale circular mirror decorated with oak leaves and surmounted by a phoenix.

The next bills are from David Garrick's house in Adelphi Terrace, which had been designed by Garrick's friend Robert Adam, so it was not surprising that Chippendale received the commission for the furniture. The main bedroom had had furniture lacquered green and yellow and red damask curtains, the drawing-room gilt-mirrors hanging on printed paper walls and curtains of green damask, while the furniture consisted of green and yellow lacquered chairs and two commodes which may have been like the ones at Nostell Priory. In the dining-room there were twelve chairs covered in red leather and studded, a mahogany table, for which Chippendale and Haig charged £10.10.0 and a side-table and pedestals. Besides supplying the furniture, Chippendale repaired pieces, and for this the charges appear very moderate. 'Fine new shelves to the inlaid presses, 10/–.' As well as the house in Adelphi Terrace, Garrick had a villa at Hampton-on-Thames, which had more furniture probably by Chippendale, and some of which is now in the Victoria and Albert Museum, notably a bed which is lacquered green and yellow. The wall-paper in the drawing-room was by Jean Pillement, a Frenchman who spent several years in England producing fantastic chinoiseries.

Chippendale also became involved with a certain Madame Cornelys, an Italian singer who had been a friend of Giacomo Casanova. This remarkable character had bought a house in Soho Square in 1767, but in 1773 she was bankrupt, which meant that Chippendale, who had been appointed an assignee of the estate, was forced to sell the contents of the house. It was noted by an American called Samuel Curwen in his *Journals and Letters* when he visited Carlisle House in 1780 that many of the furnishings were in the Chinese taste, but by this time there was a reaction against the flowery scrolls and lattice work of the Rococo, and this return to the classic was much due to architects like Robert Adam, James Wyatt, Henry Holland and Sir John Soane, and to cabinet-makers like Chippendale, Linnell, Hepplewhite and Sheraton.

66 *(left)* One of a pair of very unusual carved wood wall-brackets, with the figure of a stag. The other depicts a boar.

67 A most unusual mid-eighteenth-century gilt-wood wall-mirror with bullrush decoration and stands at the side for porcelain.

68 A late eighteenth-century bookcase with a plain pediment and doors with shaped astragals. The base is inlaid with a decoration of swags and urns.

ROBERT ADAM

ROBERT ADAM was born in 1728, the son of an architect, William Adam. He studied at Edinburgh University and then worked in his father's office, where his three other brothers were also trained. In 1754 he went to Italy and spent four years there studying the less well-known parts of classical architecture which was to prove the dominant influence in his life; for he was greatly affected by the grotesque forms of decorations which he supposed were the original and true types of classical interior decoration. These designs led Adam to create a new concept as far as both stucco work and furniture were concerned. As with the Palladian architects, he wished to create a complete understanding between the exterior and interior, and this could only be achieved if he designed every single part of the whole, from the door handles and the escutcheons to the sedan chair. As furniture is necessarily very important, so Adam gave much attention to its design, and in this he was helped by having known Piranesi while in Italy and being able to draw on his book of etchings which give details of some interiors as well as exteriors. Also there were the excavations at Pompeii and at Herculaneum. These were some of the influences under which Adam worked, and from them he was to derive a style which was his own and which was in advance of anything on the Continent. On his return from Italy in 1758, Adam was commissioned to complete the interior of Hatchlands, Admiral Boscawen's house in Surrey, and here in the dining-room he has still not developed his own style. The fireplace is of white marble and has caryatid figures supporting a plain shelf, while the ornamented mirror is framed most simply and architecturally with only an anthemion sway across the top by way of relief. This is indicative that Adam still was using antique ornament and design, even if in a more delicate fashion than previously, rather than his own more free and mature interpretations.

This work at Hatchlands led to further commissions at Shardeloes in Buckinghamshire and Croome Court in Worcestershire, while more and more work was undertaken. It is interesting to note that almost all these commissions are for alterations to existing houses, rather than for the complete construction of a new house, which is perhaps indicative that Adam was considered more highly as a renovator than as an innovator, at least as far as external work was concerned. Internally his work is

69 A half-round satinwood commode with oval decorated panels of about 1780.

70 A very fine Adam commode made of harewood inlaid with satinwood and decorated with swags and urns.

71 A fine Adam half-round harewood commode inlaid with panels of satinwood and with a painted decoration.

exquisite; for an Adam room to be completely satisfying, everything in it should be in the same genre – even the carpet should match the ceiling. Thus Adam designed, or preferred to design, not only the walls and ceilings but also the fire-irons and the fender. So suspicious was he of the tastes of his clients, that he designed the walls of the room so that only paintings of his own choice or direction could be placed thereon. He drew large panels of plasterwork which were then filled by works by his favourite artists like Angelica Kauffmann, Zucchi or Cipriani, who painted for him classical groups or romantic landscapes. This type of work was particularly remarkable at Saltram in Devon. Adam's ceiling designs were completely revolutionary and are probably his greatest achievement. In these ceilings he presented rectangles, ovals and diamonds of painting as the centres of plasterwork of the most intricate design, with leaves of acanthus and honeysuckle as well as dolphins, sphinxes and griffins. These designs were as a rule left white, while the background was painted in various soft colours. In these ceilings, and in the plasterwork on the walls, he showed great ingenuity, as did he in the shapes of the whole rooms, building in niches and other forms which had not been used before. Adam, in his *Works in Architecture*, written with his brother James, says: 'The massive entablature, the ponderous compartment ceiling, the tabernacle frame, almost the only form of ornament formerly known in this country, are now universally exploded, and in their place we have adopted a beautiful variety of light mouldings, gracefully formed, delicately enriched and arranged with propriety and skill...'

73 A detail of the commode shown in figure 70 showing the inlaid decoration.

72 *(opposite)* The dining-room at Syon House, showing the ceiling designed by Robert Adam.

The forms that Adam chose for his wall decorations, curtain-boxes and door-furniture were repeated throughout the furniture. The best way of translating this was either as marquetry or by painting. The marquetry was cut from various coloured woods, like tulipwood, kingwood or rosewood, and was then laid on a background of satinwood or harewood (which is sycamore). The commode [figure 71], which is of semi-circular form, has doors of harewood, banded with rosewood, with arabesques of satinwood let into them and the oval panels in the doors are painted with classical scenes. The frieze has a ground of satinwood, with scrolls inlaid and with a central honeysuckle motif. The top, which is again in harewood, has the main panel inlaid instead of painted. These commodes were greatly used and vary in design and material. Black lacquer was favoured and ormolu mounts were placed so as to enhance the decoration [figure 56]. Occasionally furniture was painted to match the colour-scheme of the rooms, like in the Etruscan Room at Osterley House. Some pieces were designed for a special place, and Lady Shelburne, talking of Landsdowne House, says in her diary that she went to Zucchis, where some ornaments for

51

ceilings were in preparation, and 'from there to Mayhew and Inch, where there is some beautiful cabinet-work, and two pretty glass cases for one of the rooms in my appartment, and which, though they are only deal and to be painted white, he charges £50 for'.

Although the classic was the source for much of Adam's inspiration, there are a number of pieces of furniture for which there are no known classical types, and for these Adam had to create a style of his own. This is especially true of chairs and settees where he did not use the Grecian curve but a straight or tapered leg. This support was sometimes fluted in the new style, with the leg cut concavely or reeded, which could be made with either square or circular sections. The backs were often oval with a plain wooden frame, and the only reliefs were carved paterae at the top of the leg. Adam did design chairs which are far more elaborate than the ones illustrated, but they were generally for use in a special room. The material most used was mahogany for the dining chairs, while the decorated ones were in beechwood. Settees followed the form of the chairs, with graceful sweeping backs, some of which have a carved leaf in the centre, and others are fluted.

Magnificent side-tables were made with inlaid tops similar in drawing to the commode [figure 71], standing on tapering gilt legs, or with caryatid supports. These were used in the dining-room too, where the tops were made of marble or mosaic; the inlay was either with geometric or classical pattern. These inlaid marbles add great richness and colour, for lapis-lazuli and malachite were mixed with Derbyshire spar and many others. In the dining-room, besides these tables, Adam often placed sideboards, supported on either side by two pedestals sur-

75 A mahogany candlestand of about 1765.

76 Adam's design for the gallery in Syon House.

77 Adam's design for the ceiling of the dining-room at Syon House.

78 A blue John and ormolu candelabrum made by William Boulton in about 1780.

mounted by urns. These urns were used for keeping bottles or as plate warmers. These were made *en suite* and with them there was sometimes a cellaret made of the same wood and with the same decoration.

Pedestals and torcherons, the first which supported vases or statuary and the second which supported candles, were designed both in the purely classical manner and in Adam's freer adaptation. Most of the latter are in carved wood with ram's head or caryatid mask ornamentation, standing directly on the ground on the favourite hoof feet, or on a raised plinth. Another form of lighting was by means of candelabra or a wall-bracket, or through girandoles, which, having mirror-plates, increased the light given by the candles.

Mirrors tended to be incorporated with the plasterwork and quite a number were made with composition frames. The ornamental mirror was greatly used with human figure supports, griffins' and rams' heads being the most frequent decorations. Pier-mirrors were made to go over the side-tables already described, and these often consisted of a plain gilt frame with only a curved cresting.

Among the cabinet-makers who worked for Adam were Chippendale, Samuel Norman, William France and his partner Beckwith, and John Linnell, who was a draughtsman of considerable merit. Chippendale is known to have worked at Harewood House where Adam did the drawings for the interior between 1765 and 1771, and the standard of craftsmanship is probably higher than anything Chippendale had previously attained. The marquetry furniture is magnificent and it is also extremely fine at Panshanger in Hertfordshire, where there is a pair of china cabinets of great beauty. Samuel Norman is known to have worked for Sir Lawrence Dundas, for whom Adam

79 A serpentine Coromandel lacquer commode.

80 A satinwood window seat with shaped ends.

designed a set of chairs and a settee, and these Norman probably made. William France made furniture for Lord Mansfield at Kenwood, and on the bill which is at the Victoria and Albert Museum there is an item which France says was made 'from Mr Adam's design', namely 'two very rich frames for your tables with eight legs to each, richly carved ornaments under the rails finished in a masterly manner and mouldings also and sweep'd stretching rails glued up four times £67.12.0'. John Linnell worked for William Drake at Shardeloes and also for Sir Nathaniel Curzon at Kedleston, and there exist drawings by both Adam and Linnell which compare with sofas still in the house.

Among those who disapproved of Adam's style and work were Samuel Johnson who, on visiting Kedleston in 1774, noted that 'the grandeur was all below' and that 'the bedchambers were small low and dark, and fitter for a prison than for a house of splendour'; and Horace Walpole who, referring to Mrs Child's bed at Osterley, said that it was 'too theatric, and too like a modern head-dress, for round the outside of the dome are festoons of artificial flowers. What would Vitruvius think of a dome decorated by a milliner?' Generally, however, the style was admired and copied not only by architects but by cabinet-makers during the last twenty-five years of the century.

GEORGE HEPPLEWHITE

82　A rare show-wood frame armchair with a gadrooned back, seat-rail and legs.

GEORGE HEPPLEWHITE'S fame rests on the publication of *The Cabinet Maker and Upholsterer's Guide*, which was undertaken by his widow two years after his death. The title ends 'from drawings by A. Hepplewhite and Co. cabinet-makers', but it is by no means certain that he was responsible for the drawings. Apart from this book, little is known about the man except that he was apprenticed to the firm of Gillow of Lancaster, and later set up shop in Redcross Street, Cripplegate. There is no single piece of furniture that can definitely be ascribed to Hepplewhite, nor is there any evidence that he was patronized by any great person. A year after the publication of the first edition of the *Cabinet Maker's Guide*, a second was printed and then in 1794 a third and 'improved' edition appeared. As Sheraton had commented prior to the last edition, that 'this work had already caught the decline', it may be that this remark prompted the authors to change some of the designs. However, this was the first large trade directory to appear for over twenty years and as it contains about three hundred pieces, it needs consideration at some length.

The development of furniture during the last twenty-five years of the century owed much to Adam's neo-classicism, and in this the drawings from Hepplewhite's book are not exceptional. Most of the furniture illustrated is inlaid on satinwood, with marquetry of many different woods. It is true that very elegant pieces were made at this time, especially small tables and chairs, but the object of the book was as much to aid the country craftsman as to affect the city cabinet-maker.

The name of Hepplewhite has come to be synonymous with a type of chair that was very popular at the end of the eighteenth century, which we now call a shield-back. In the first edition of the *Guide*, there are twenty-four separate drawings for chairs of this kind, including four which are described as 'Cabriole Chairs'. The opening remarks concern the dimensions of the chairs generally and it is recommended that they should be 'width in the front 20 inches, depth of the seat 17 inches, height of the seat frame 17 inches, total height about 3 feet 1 inch', but the author adds that they are 'frequently adapted according to the size of the room, or the pleasure of the purchaser'.

Chairs were generally made of mahogany and might be covered in 'horse-hair, plain, striped, chequered, etc., at pleasure'.

81　*(opposite)* A fine satinwood cabinet inlaid with panels of *pietra-dura*.

There was apparently a new fashion for painting and lacquering chairs, for there is a whole paragraph devoted to them, pointing out specimens which were particularly well adapted to that style. A chair, in fact made in mahogany, but very closely resembling one of these drawings, is illustrated [figure 85]. It was suggested that these decorated chairs should be covered in linen or cotton 'to accord with the general hue of the chair'.

In most cases the shield part of the back is plain with the decoration extending only occasionally to the shield itself. The interior of the shield was made with a centre splat, pierced and either plain in the country-made chairs, or very variously carved. The most popular motifs were the Prince of Wales' feathers, the wheat-ear, the classical urn or hanging drapery. These were most ingeniously worked sometimes nearly to fill the shield, while in others the splat is narrow and contains only two shaped bars. Chairs with oval backs and heart-shaped backs were made and an example of the latter is illustrated [figure 88], and these seem to have been popular; square-backed chairs are illustrated in the first edition of the *Guide*, but were probably not fashionable until the last decade of the eighteenth century. The shield-

83 A pair of shield-shaped backed armchairs in mahogany of 1785 to 1790.

84 Hepplewhite's design for the chair shown in figure 85, published in *The Cabinet Maker and Upholsterer's Guide*, 1787.

85 A Hepplewhite oval-backed armchair with a motif of Prince of Wales' feathers.

backed chair was made with an upholstered back and many of these survive, both in sets and in single examples; a specially fine one is illustrated [figure 83], and has most finely carved gadrooned mouldings to the legs, seat-frame and back. Hepplewhite calls these chairs 'cabriole' though why they were so called is not known. Only one of the six shield-backed chairs illustrated has a French leg and this is on a page on which the chairs are not described as cabriole.

Chair legs were usually straight and tapered, either square-

86 A mahogany commode in the French style with very fine mounts.

shaped, fluted or moulded in the Adam tradition, but occasionally the end of the leg curved outwards. The knee was carved or decorated with paterae or tusks, and the seat-rail was often shaped, either serpentined or bowed. On the finest examples, the carving and shaping show to great effect. There are also three designs for hall chairs, which according to Hepplewhite are 'much improved'. The type which is most often seen has either a more shaped or oval back and a solid wooden seat. The centre of the back has a coat-of-arms painted on it but the rest of the chair is plain. In none of the designs, except for a type of winged chair called a 'Saddle-check or easy chair', are there any stretchers. These were added by country makers, for they strengthened the construction even if they detracted from its line.

There are five drawings for stools and six for window stools in the first edition of the *Guide*, and it is suggested that they be made and covered in the same materials as the chairs, with a preference for mahogany and japanning and 'taberray' or morin, of a pea-green or other light colour. A French leg is drawn, similar to the one on the 'cabriole' chair, for three of the four stools, and a number of these pieces survive with both serpentine and straight seat-rails. The fifth stool is called a 'gouty stool' which stands on four plain square legs and has a top which may be altered in height and angle. The window stools were made to stand close to the wall under the window and therefore depended for size and proportion on the window but 'their heights should not exceed the seats of the chairs'. All the six stools illustrated have straight, tapering legs – either square or round, but examples exist, dating from the 1780's, with the curved French leg. The seats of these pieces are all upholstered and the seat-rail is exposed and carved with various motifs, while in one

87 A rare supper table of oak and mahogany with a wire grill cage of about 1770.

example the seat-rail has material gathered in rouches, hung from it. Two particularly fine examples are those on fluted tapering legs and decorated in gilt.

The next section of the *Guide* is devoted to sofas and of these, five have upholstered seats and backs, while the sixth is a chair-backed one, with four splatted shield-shaped sections. This is described as 'of modern invention', but the general principle is the same as the chair-backed settees of the early eighteenth century. The first four designs are similar to many of the most elegant chairs, in that they have flowing graceful lines to the back, and stand on tapering legs. Hepplewhite suggests that they should be between six and seven feet in length, and about thirty inches in depth, while the height of the backs corresponds to the height recommended for chairs, three feet one inch. A few smaller settees, of about five feet, were made but these are uncommon. There are drawings for a 'Confidante' and a 'Duchesse', which were both popular in France at the time. The first consists of a large settee with a chair added to each end, and the drawing is very similar to the one illustrated [figure 97] which is decorated in gilt. The second is a sofa made up of two *bergère* chairs with a stool in the centre and may be used in the drawing-room or bedroom; it was the forerunner of the day-bed which became so very popular during the first decade of the nineteenth century.

The popularity of sideboards and side-tables increased greatly at the end of the eighteenth century and two distinct types were made. The first and more practical type has a centre drawer in

88 *(below left)* An unusual heart-shaped backed mahogany armchair.

89 *(below centre)* An oval-backed armchair with a show-wood frame on cabriole legs.

90 *(below right)* A mahogany oval-backed armchair with a show-wood frame on tapering, reeded legs.

92 A mahogany library drum-table with lettered
drawers and a centre section for holding money.

91 A Hepplewhite mahogany chair with a
pierced back and an unusual circular form.

the frieze and a deep drawer at either side. One of these has
wine compartments for bottles and a space behind these for
'cloths or napkins the whole depth of the drawer'; while the
other side is divided into two drawers, one lined in green baize
to hold plate, the other lined in lead 'for the convenience of
holding water to wash glasses etc. – there must be a valve-cork
or plug at the bottom, to let off the dirty water'. The centre
drawer was also used for keeping table linen. A mahogany sideboard of this type is well worth mentioning; the banding is
rosewood, the top is serpentine-shaped and there is a drawer
above the shaped central arch. The second type was a side-table
without drawers, which was designed for use with a pair of
supporting urns on stands. These tables were usually straight-
fronted and supported by four legs, but in the example in the
Guide there are six legs and a far more elaborate frieze. These
friezes were inlaid with many types of wood like rosewood,
harewood (which is sycamore), kingwood, tulipwood and
satinwood, or painted with classical motifs of sways or festoons
of flowers, urns, paterae and honeysuckle. Marble tops were
used but not so often as in Adam designs. The example illustrated
[figure 104] is in mahogany with a shaped top and frieze, which
is supported by two mouldings. The mahogany panels of the
frieze are banded in satinwood and the legs are fluted, ending
in a square, tapering toe, while the ends are square. Tables of
this kind were made from five feet to seven feet in length and
were often placed in recesses which were made for them. This

63

93 A pair of Rococo gilt-wood wall brackets of about 1760.

seems to have been the case in the grander dining-room, for they were usually made *en suite* with a pair of pedestals and vases, one of which served as a plate-warmer, being provided with racks and a stand for a heater and is lined with strong tin; the other pedestal is used as a pot-cupboard. The vases which surmounted these pedestals were used for holding water for the use of the butler, or iced water for drinking, enclosed in an inner partition, with ice surrounding it, or for knife cases. These pieces of furniture were most finely made with inlaid panels of painted or inlaid wood. The pedestals were designed to be the same height as the side-table and from sixteen to eighteen inches square. The vases were about twenty-seven inches high, and only the larger dining-room could take this form of sideboard.

Two other pieces of furniture were also popular: the cellaret and the knife box. The first was usually made of mahogany and

95 A mahogany secretaire bookcase with a pierced swan-necked pediment.

94 One of Hepplewhite's designs for the top of a Pembroke table.

96 Hepplewhite's drawing for a confidante consisting of a settee with a chair added to each end.

banded in brass for strength and decoration. The interior was divided like the bottle drawer of the first type of sideboard, and was lined in lead. They were either oval or octagonal in shape and stood on tapering squared legs. These pieces were placed either near or under the side-table. The knife boxes were made to be placed either on the side-table or on pedestals. They were again usually pieces of fine quality and were made in 'satin or other light coloured wood'; the decoration was mostly inlay but painted examples are found. These pieces were first designed by Adam, who was much interested in making the design of dining-rooms more important, for as he said; 'the eating rooms are considered as the apartments of conversation, in which we pass a great part of our time'.

Considerable prominence is also given to pieces for the library, notably bureau-bookcases, desks and secretaire-bookcases. They were 'usually made of good mahogany'. The bureau-bookcase was popular and was produced in large numbers. The top part was given variety by different types of glazing bar and by ornamenting the top with a 'scroll of foliage, a vase, a bust or other ornament, which may be of mahogany, or gilt, or of a light coloured wood'. The proportions do not show great variety, varying in width from about three feet six inches to four feet three inches, in height from three feet two inches to three feet five inches, and length from about six feet to seven feet three inches, depending on the size and height of the room. The base

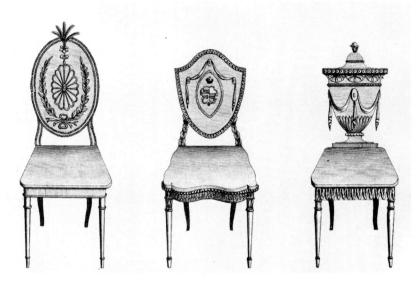

98 Three drawings for hall chairs by Hepplewhite and published in his *Guide*.

either consisted of a cupboard or a series of drawers. The fall always enclosed small drawers and pigeon-holes. The secretaire-bookcase followed very similar principles except that instead of a fall-front on which to write, the top drawer pulled out, the front hinged down and was fixed 'by means of a spring and quadrant'. The base either had drawers or sliding shelves for keeping clothes, implying that this piece could be used in the bedroom. Desks or library-tables were most simple in appearance and were usually made of mahogany, with no ornamentation or ormolu mounts, the sole concession being that the top was covered in coloured leather or cloth. They either had drawers which ran half-way back and thus could be used by two people, or one side had drawers and the other cupboards. In exceptional cases, the desk might have shaped ends or decoration down the sides of the drawers or cupboards, but these forms

97 A confidante similar to the drawing in Hepplewhite's *Guide*. The ends were adapted from *bergère* chairs.

Design for a Bed.

101 A gilt-wood torchère with a ram's head
decoration and glass candleholders.

100 A rosewood occasional table on square,
tapering legs of about 1790.

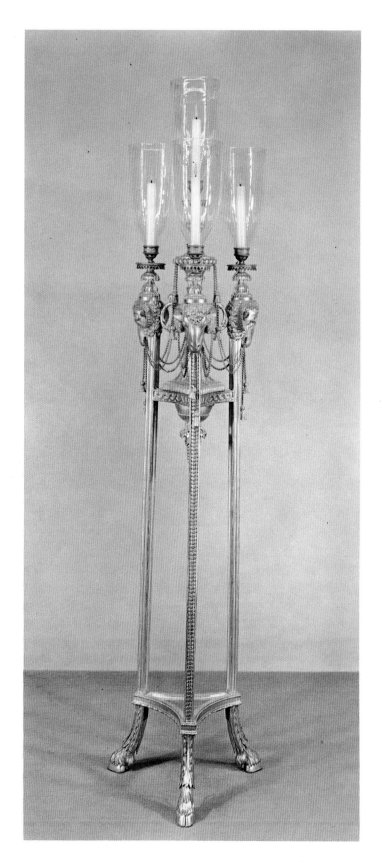

99 (opposite) A design for a bed from the *Guide*,
with a petticoat valance and the dome which
appears in all the designs for beds.

102 A very rare mahogany secretaire with tambour-shaped drawers of about 1770.

103 Three drawings for pedestals and vases from Hepplewhite's *Guide*.

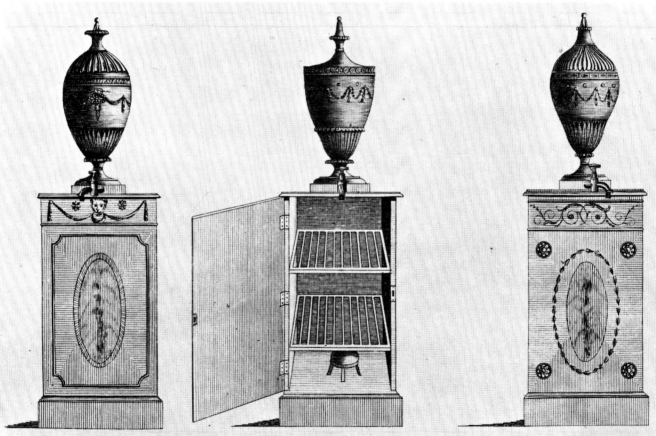

104 A mahogany shaped-front side-table with a fluted frieze and legs and gadrooned moulding.

are rare. Bookcases [figure 95] could be made in satinwoods but were more common in mahogany, with the panels inlaid in various woods. The side panels could be extended so that the whole piece might reach ten feet in width or even more. The centre part often contained a secretaire drawer which surmounted either a cupboard or drawers, while a similar arrangement of alternate drawers and cupboards was continued either side. The top was reserved for the keeping of books, with glazed doors enclosing shelves, and the pediment could be topped by an urn or a broken arch.

Chests-of-drawers and commodes feature in the *Guide* and are described as 'dressing drawers' and 'commodes'. The first are more diverse than the second and are serpentine [figure 108] or bow-fronted and have the top drawer fitted with compartments and a mirror, occasionally with a brushing slide between the top drawer and the top of the chest. The authors say in describing the chest with serpentine front 'the drawers to which are elegantly ornamented with inlaid or painted work, which is applied with great beauty and elegance to this piece of furniture'. These chests are especially pleasing in satinwood but are more common in mahogany. The 'chest-of-drawers' is a plainer piece of rectangular shape with three long and two short drawers. The commode is 'adapted for a drawing-room...and being used in principal rooms, requires considerable elegance'. It is most often made in satinwood and is inlaid on the doors and top in many different woods. This piece may be of many shapes, but the most common are the half-round and the serpentine-fronted. The one illustrated [figure 69] is in satinwood with a circular painted panel on the centre door, in the classical manner, while the panels on the side doors are oval. The doors are cross-banded in rosewood, as is the top which has a painted border of entwined flowers and ribbons. The other commode [figure 115]

105 A half-round side-table in gilt with a floral designed top.

106 *(opposite)* An oval backed gilt-wood armchair on fluted, tapering legs.

offers an interesting contrast, relying more on the boldness of the inlay rather than on the painting for its effect, with the satinwood standing out strongly against the harewood background.

Tables of many interesting designs are drawn, among them the 'Pembroke' which became increasingly favoured, and the pier-table. These are both smaller than the dining-room side-tables as a rule, and could therefore be placed in many rooms. The Pembroke had two flaps and was most often rectangular or

108 A serpentine-fronted chest-of-drawers made of satinwood in about 1785.

107 An inlaid satinwood and mahogany card-table on tapering legs.

oval in shape and stood on tapering square or oval legs. The tops were inlaid either on a mahogany, satinwood or hare-wood ground, with arabesques or geometrical patterns of marquetry. There is a fine example in satinwood and is of serpentine shape, with a banding of rosewood inlaid with circular pieces of satinwood. The oval panels in the top and sides are of rosewood inlaid with harewood and satinwood. These pieces were made to stand free in a room but are admirable also when placed against a sofa. Pier-tables were not put to such general use as Pembroke tables, for they had to stand against the wall, and so they could 'admit, with great propriety, of much elegance and ornament'. They were made especially to stand under mirrors with, in certain cases, the mirrors resting on the top of the table, and so they are liable to be higher than other tables. There are illustrated four such tables and also four separate tops of different and fine design, variously shaped from the elliptical to the al-most rectangular. These tops are all either to be inlaid or painted and made to stand on tapering square, round or cabriole legs, of which there is an example which has a gilded base with shaped frieze: the top is of inlaid satinwood and has around it a gadrooned ormolu band.

Occasional tables were made in great variety and profusion during the last twenty years of the eighteenth century. The continuing habit of drinking tea accounted for many of these for it became customary for each person to have a table of his own from which to eat and drink. By this time the price of tea had dropped and also the 'thé' had become fashionable. This form of entertaining came from France where large numbers of people used to sit down to tea or coffee at eight o'clock. Besides these tea or urn-tables, there were small writing tables of the

109 A fine Hepplewhite harewood secretaire cabinet on
cabriole legs and inlaid with
satinwood.

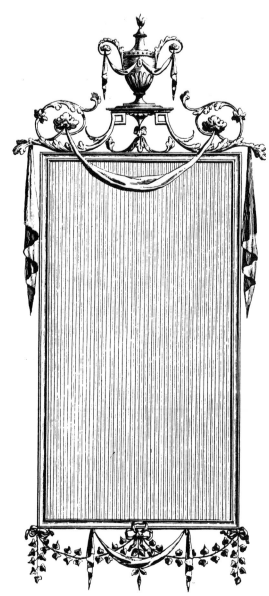

110 A design for a mirror with the classical motifs of an urn and festoons of drapery.

type often found which is in burr-elm and has a tray below which joins the shaped tapering legs together. The drawer opens from the side and across the front there is a slide on which to write a note. There were many card-tables inlaid in a manner similar to the Pembroke table and the pier-table and which were half-round in shape, but others exist from this time of bold experiment and design in plain mahogany. The insides of these tables were usually covered in baize, but some have a wooden interior.

The producers of the *Guide* are much concerned with beds which they regard as 'articles of much importance as well on account of the great expense attending them, as the variety of shapes, and the high degree of elegance which may be shown in them'. They advise that valances should be tied up in festoons or gathered full in what was known as the Petticoat valance. Any materials might be used and 'white dimity', 'printed cottons' and 'Manchester stuffs' were thought suitable. All the beds have posts at the head and foot and are domed. The corners could be in 'carved mahogany, gilded, painted or japanned', and 'the ornaments over the cornice, may be in the same manner... will produce the most lively effect'. Other forms of decorations were stuffed head-boards with arms or other ornaments carved and gilded.

Girandoles and mirrors followed closely on Adam designs and were most highly carved with the classical motifs of the urn, festoons of drapery, pendant tusks and the eagle with spread wings. The borders of these mirrors, both round and rectangular, consisted of a plain frame with enrichments on the top and spreading from the bottom. They were largely drawn to go over tables or commodes placed between windows, but tended to become more stylized and dependent on the decoration of the room, although it is stated in the *Guide* that 'they may be carved and coloured suitable to the room'. Glass remained expensive, especially in large sheets, but the rest of the pieces of furniture were not excessively priced. The cabinet-makers' *London Book of Prices*, which contains drawings by Hepplewhite and Thomas Shearer, quotes prices on card-tables from 7/6 to 15/–, on Pembroke tables from 10/6 to £1.8.0 and on a Carlton House writing table for £8.0.0.

It must not be supposed that Hepplewhite produced great quantities of furniture himself. His importance lies in the collection of drawings made in the *Guide*. Among the most important cabinet-makers working at the time were Seddon, Thomas Chippendale the Younger and Gillows. The first-named had premises in Aldersgate Street where he employed eighty craftsmen in 1768, when the building was destroyed by fire. By 1789 his stock in trade was worth £118,900, with timber stocks at £24,000, upholstery at £3,000 and carpets at £9,000. In the diary of a

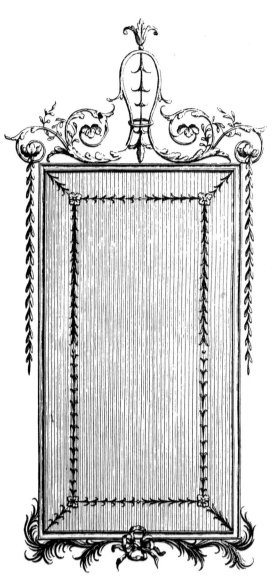

111 Another of Hepplewhite's designs for mirrors showing the plain, narrow frame and the enrichments on the top and bottom.

He employs four hundred apprentices on any work connected with the making of household furniture – joiners, carvers, gilders, mirror-makers, upholsterers, girdlers – who mould the bronze into graceful patterns – and locksmiths. All these are housed in a building with six wings. In the basement mirrors are cast and cut. Some other department contains nothing but chairs, sofas and stools of every description, some quite simple, others exquisitely carved and made of all varieties of wood, and one large room is full up with all the finished articles in this line, while others are occupied by writing-tables, cupboards, chests-of-drawers, charmingly fashioned desks, chests, both large and small, work and toilet-tables in all manner of woods and patterns, from the simplest and cheapest to the most elegant and expensive...

Chintz, silk and wool materials for curtains and bedcovers; hangings in every possible material; carpets and stair-carpets to order; in short, anything one might desire to furnish a house; and all the workmen besides and a great many seamstresses; their own saw-house too, where as many blocks of fine foreign wood lie piled, as firs and oak are seen at our saw-mills. The entire story of the wood, as used for both inexpensive and costly furniture, and the method of treating it, can be traced in this establishment.

Seddon, foster-father to four hundred employees, seemed to me a respectable man, a man of genius, too, with an understanding for the needs of the needy and the luxurious; knowing how to satisfy them from the products of nature and the artistry of manufacture; a man who has become intimate with the quality of woods from all parts of the earth, with the chemical knowledge of how to colour them or combine their own tints with taste, has appreciated the value of all his own people's labour and toil, and is for ever creating new forms.

It is interesting to note the number of specialized branches of furniture-making that Seddon undertook, especially the making of ormolu mounts and the glass-making. Mathew Boulton (1728–1809), who with James Watt produced an improved steam engine with a rotary motion in 1781, was a man with wide-spread interests, among them the making of fine ormolu. He, with another Midland iron-master John Williamson, helped with the improvement of roads by exerting pressure on the Turnpike Trusts and so, with better communications, metalwork became cheaper. This in turn helped the makers in England, for they could then compete with the French who until this time had had a virtual monopoly. Glass-making became cheaper and a new process was introduced from France in 1773.

The firm of Gillow built premises in what was then called Oxford Road, now Oxford Street, during the early 1770's, although their main workshops continued to be in Lancaster, the pieces being sent down by sea. The firm was well-known for being inexpensive and supplying good craftsmanship. A German visitor P. A. Nemmich comments in 1807, 'their work is good and solid though not of the first class in inventiveness and style.'

After the death of Thomas Chippendale in 1779, the firm continued with his son and Haig as partners until Haig retired in 1796. During the years 1796 and 1797, Chippendale was employed by Lord Harewood in Yorkshire and in London. The quality of craftsmanship was maintained and some very fine pieces in the Regency style survive at Harewood and Stanhead. In 1804 the firm went bankrupt and the stock in trade was sold by auction, including '...commodes, chiffoniers, chests-of-drawers, sofas, card, writing and several sets of dining and breakfast tables.' However the firm continued to trade until at least 1820. The younger Chippendale died in 1822.

112 A pair of late eighteenth-century japanned chairs with a decoration of draperies and classical motifs.

THOMAS SHERATON

113 A design for a cabinet from Sheraton's *Cabinet-makers' and Upholsterers' Drawing Book,* published in 1791.

THOMAS SHERATON was born at Stockton-on-Tees in 1751 and came to London during the early years of the 1790's. Although he was a carver and cabinet-maker by trade and describes himself as a 'mechanic', it is almost certain that during his life in London he produced no furniture himself, being engaged more in designing and publishing besides preaching as a Baptist. He published the *Cabinet-makers' and Upholsterers' Drawing Book* in 1791–1794, which consists of three parts with an appendix and an accompaniment. The first two parts are devoted to geometrical designs and are of no great interest to us, although the author thought them most important. Part 3 'is intended to exhibit the present taste of furniture, and at the same time, to give the workmen some assistance in the manufacturing part of it'. He also made various comments on the work of some of his predecessors, saying of Chippendale that 'his designs are now wholly antiquated and laid aside', of Manwaring that his book has nothing 'but what an apprentice boy may be taught by seven hours proper instruction', and of Hepplewhite that 'if we compare some of the designs, particularly the chairs, with the newest taste, we shall find that this work has already caught the decline and perhaps, in a little while, will suddenly die in the disorder'.

This 'new design' showed that Sheraton drew his inspiration from the type of furniture being produced in France at the end of the reign of Louis XVI and during the early years of the Directoire. But although he certainly studied French furniture, some of which no doubt had been appearing in London since 1790, his designs remained individual, as by 1802 he is complaining that 'a clumsy fourfooted stool from France will be admired by our connoisseurs in preference to a first-rate cabinet of English production', and that 'when our tradesmen are desirous to draw the best customers to their ware-rooms they hasten over to Paris, or otherwise pretend to go there, plainly indicating at our defects in cabinet-making, or extreme ignorance, that we must be pleased and attracted by the mere sound of French taste'.

It is noticeable in his chair designs, as for many other pieces, that Sheraton preferred straight lines to curves and concentrated on square backs rather than on the ovals, heart shaped or shield-backs so well exemplified by Hepplewhite. These backs were divided as a rule into three parts with the centre third filled with one of the normal classical motifs such as a festoon of drapery, a vase or the wheat-ear. The division into three sections was fairly rigidly adhered to, especially in what Sheraton calls 'parlour chairs' which were also straight-fronted, and differed in this from 'drawing-room chairs', which had shaped seats. The top and bottom rails of the chairs were usually straight and narrow, but could have a centre raised panel. This panel was usually raised straight from the back rail, but there are some curved examples. Legs were either square or round and tapering, with surfaces reeded or fluted and sometimes spiralling. During the last ten years of the century it is more common to find chair and table legs with reeded rather than fluted supports, which

114 A gilt-wood settee on shaped legs and with a finely carved seat-rail.

115 A half-round commode made of mahogany, satinwood and harewood in about 1780.

although possibly stronger, do not give such elegance of line. The arms were slightly shaped from the joint with the backs and then came forward to a straight or tapering support brought either from the top of the leg or from slightly in on the seat-rail. Another form of arm support, which was sometimes reeded, curved from the top of the front to the fore-ends of the arm. Sheraton says that the number of reeds should be uneven and there 'should be one on the centre facing the eye'. The material used was most commonly mahogany, but a large number of chairs were made in beechwood, with decoration in painting and gilt, with panels of *grisaille* in the backs, and on these the backs and seats could be caned. The designs for both types of chair were much the same. The drawing-room chair tended to be grander with decoration in gold, and the seats were sometimes covered in tapestry like their French counterparts. Settees were much in fashion, and those of this period are specially graceful following the lines of chair design. Carving was again used for the backs, and was sometimes inset with panels of wood painted

81

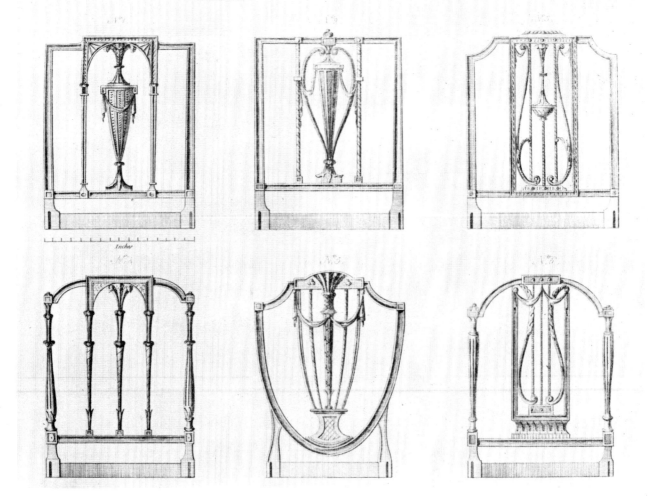

116 Six designs for chair backs from Sheraton's book, showing his preference for square backs.

with the same decoration as the legs and rails. Sheraton only shows two drawings for settees in the *Drawing Book* and both are upholstered. The seats are covered in material and bolsters could be used at each end, a fashion which was to continue for the first twenty years of the nineteenth century. Surprisingly, there are no designs for stools or for window seats, but examples from this period follow the principles of the previous decade in that they closely resemble the chairs. There are, however, two drawings for *chaise-longues* which like the *Duchesse* and the *bergère* were found in fashionable drawing-rooms, and were used 'to rest or loll upon after dinner'.

Small tables of great variety were introduced during the 1790's, some with French influence and some of novel design. The tripod support was again fashionable, but more lightly handled than during the middle of the century, and the inward turned leg ended in either a plain tapering toe or with a ball. The support was often vase-shaped, decorated with japanning or carving, while the top was circular, square, hexagonal or oval, and could be tilted so as to be placed out of the way. Oc-

casional tables were also made standing on four slender tapering supports and fitted with small drawers, pen-trays and ink-wells, as well as writing-slides and small slides. The tops of these tables were often filled with ratchets and a removable bar so that they could be used for reading. Sheraton illustrates a number of designs for fire-screens, both on tripod bases and straight supports. A number of both types survive. The former were usually in satinwood or japanned, and had a shield-shaped movable plaque on a long stem, adjustable to keep the heat from the face. The latter were less often painted, and were fitted on occasions as a writing desk, with one side hanging down. A number of small work-tables were produced, some on the lines of the writing tables but with the drawer fitted with compartments for needles with bobbins for silk and with pin-cushions; others were similar to the French *tricoteuse* and had a tray top, hinged on one side, opened by a thumbspring. These had a second shelf used to hold the sewing but this was not enclosed. These pieces are usually in satinwood or mahogany rather plainly and strongly made, and in this they differ from the French examples, which were most beautifully inlaid and were pieces of great elegance. One may suppose, therefore, that the English examples were seldom used in the drawing-room.

Pembroke tables were made in large quantities, most often in satinwood decorated with japanning or in mahogany. They stood on tapering, either plain or reeded, supports, with the tops either rectangular or oval. They were also popular, according to Sheraton, 'to breakfast upon'. There is also a design for what Sheraton calls a 'Harlequin Pembroke table' which has a series of

117 A late eighteenth-century side chair with typical japanned decoration.

118 A late eighteenth-century settee, the back rail of which is japanned.

119 An unusual satinwood
and marbleized roll-topped
secretaire on tapering legs.

120 *(opposite)* A satinwood secretaire cabinet
84 with shaped astragals and cornices.

drawers made to rise out of the top, converting the table into a
desk. These nests of drawers can be either oval or rectangular,
not depending on the shape of the table, and can be lowered by
pressing two thumb pieces. Sheraton admits that this table was
not an invention of his own, but that a friend gave him the idea
for the drawing. These tables are not very practical, for they
are necessarily short of drawers, but they show great ingenuity.
The sofa-table, a form of Pembroke table, was introduced during
this period, and two are illustrated [figures 127 and 134].

121 A pair of Sheraton corner stools. The decoration is painted onto them.

122 Two of Sheraton's designs for *chaise-longues* which were very fashionable at that time.

Games tables for the playing of chess and backgammon were also made varying in size from about 1′6″ square to the size of the normal Pembroke table. The top may be slid off and turned over, revealing the chess board, while the backgammon board is hidden below, but occasionally the chess board remained always in view.

Pier- or side-tables were made to serve purely ornamental purposes, and so were lightly and gracefully made. The tops were made of marble which might be inlaid or painted, or they were 'recessed in satinwood or rosewood with a cross-band on the outside, a border about two inches richly japanned, and a narrow cross-band beyond it, to go all round'. The bases were in gold or white and gilt with a carved frieze and centre plaque, the legs tapering with gold or white and gold and carved enrichments, while stretchers were occasionally added joining at the top of the toe with a central urn enhancing the rich effect. These tables were either shallow rectangular-shaped with curved ends, standing on four or six legs, or elliptical or half-round.

Sheraton designed a large number of pieces of furniture for writing, some of which are original in design, but most of which followed the general principles of the previous decade. The bureau or secretaire bookcase, which occasionally has a cylinder or roll-top concealing the writing section, was much made and two examples are illustrated [figures 119 and 120]. The lower part contains both the writing drawer and either further drawers or cupboards, while the top section is glazed, with shaped 'astragals', and is surmounted by a plain pediment. At this time the pediment was rarely shaped. These pieces are made both in mahogany and satinwood and are usually cross-banded, to add to the painting or the figure of the wood. Sheraton illustrates a larger bookcase, which has no writing section, in five parts, the centre three projecting beyond the two end ones. In this drawing he has taken great pains to emphasize the importance of the choice of wood for the door panels. There is a drawing for a kidney-shaped writing table of a type which was to be made in numbers during the nineteenth century; the tiers of five drawers were arranged on either side of a kneehole, the top of which has

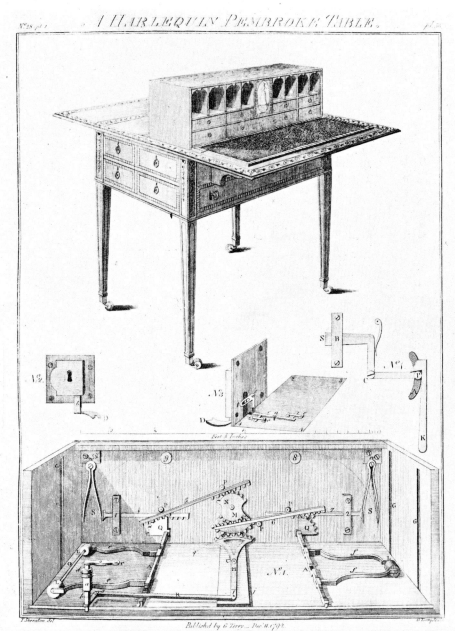

123 Sheraton's design for his 'Harlequin Pembroke table' showing the mechanism which allowed the drawers to be raised, converting the table into a desk.

124 *(opposite)* A late eighteenth-century yellow painted commode with panels in the manner of Angelica Kauffmann.

a slide for holding a book and is shaped 'like that intestine part of animals'. Another type of table which was popular at the period and was described in the *Drawing Book* as a 'Ladies' Drawing and Writing Table', has since become known as a 'Carlton House table', although there is no proof that the Prince of Wales ordered one or admired the design. One in mahogany, standing on square tapering legs, the top part consisting of drawers and cupboards, is illustrated in figure 128. Another of Sheraton's drawings for an oval library-table, a copy of which has 'already

125 A rare ivory and ebony chair on tapering legs and with a plain splatted back of about 1785.

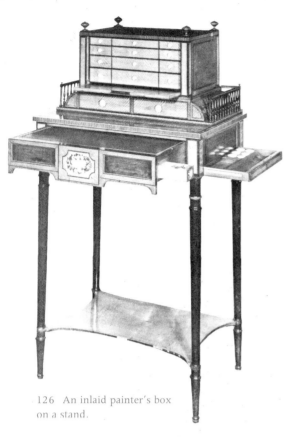

126 An inlaid painter's box on a stand.

been executed for the Duke of York', had to be made in mahogany with carved decoration, its only relief apart from the use of brass mouldings, which had only recently regained favour. The doors enclosed either cupboards or drawers or divisions for large books, and the piece has the merit of adding a new shape to the library, although the design is not very practical.

Besides the 'Carlton House table', Sheraton illustrates other writing cabinets specially for the use of ladies. These pieces are usually small and made of satinwood, harewood or mahogany. One which is frequently found has a roll-topped writing part surmounted by a glazed section which was to have 'green silk fluting behind the glass and drapery put on at top'. Another type sometimes known as a *bonheur du jour* has a hinged top, lined with either leather or silk, which, when in use, folds over and is either held firm by two runners or by opening the long drawer in the frame. The drawers in the cabinet are either open, or concealed by another fall and are often surmounted by a bookshelf. It is interesting to note that Sheraton says that the bureau with the fall-front and drawers to the ground was not often made in London, but was still made 'very frequently' in the country, showing that pieces of that type were made during the whole of the century.

Commodes remained important pieces of drawing-room furniture and became increasingly elaborate. There is one illustrated in the Appendix of the *Drawing Book* which has four doors,

127 An unusual sofa-table made of rosewood on shaped supports, about 1795.

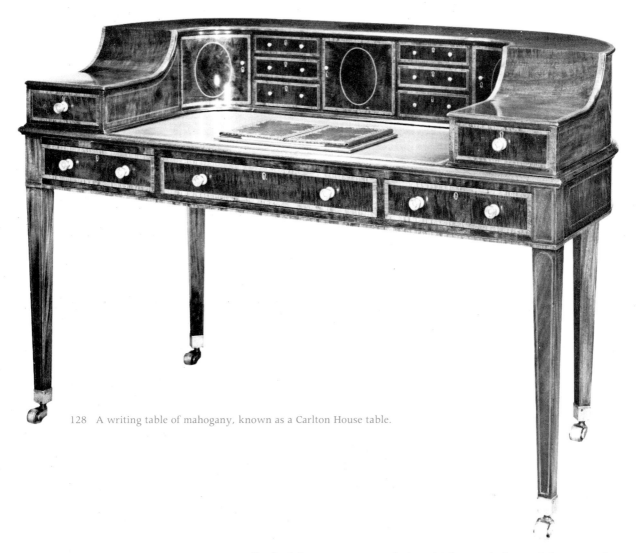

128   A writing table of mahogany, known as a Carlton House table.

flanked by two open ends in which stand classical figures. The piece stands on spiral column legs which are placed in either side of the outside doors. The top is of marble and has a pier mirror resting on it as well as two candelabra and a clock. Commodes of this kind are usually in satinwood with panels inlaid with other exotic woods or figures painted in the classical manner. The general principle of a commode continues to be that of an enclosed pier-table, and was considered for the same purpose – namely decoration.

It was fashionable for bedsteads of this period to have simple and reeded tapering bedposts, reaching a vase form, which is carved, standing on plain square supports. The draperies were still of great importance and Sheraton designed many valances which are extremely elaborate, to go with beds also of the wildest fancy, and called by him an 'Elliptic Bed for a single Lady', a 'French State Bed' and a 'Summer Bed in two Compartments' which was designed 'so that two people might sleep separately

129 A very fine satinwood and painted cabinet with a shaped top, secretaire drawer and cupboards.

130. *(opposite)* A Queen Anne burr-elm bureau bookcase.

in hot weather'. In this design the two beds are joined at the feet by an arch with a passage-way between.

Other pieces of furniture that Sheraton designed for the bedroom include two dressing chests which have shaped fronts, and reeded columns on either side. One has a brushing slide and the other is drawn with the top drawer open revealing many compartments and a writing flap or looking-glass. Sheraton says that these two pieces were designed on a new plan, and they differ from earlier pieces in that the wood used is satinwood as

131 Sheraton's designs for his two dressing chests. The top one is drawn with top drawer open, revealing a writing flap and many compartments. The bottom one has a brushing slide.

often as mahogany, the top drawer is more fully fitted and the shape previously used was more often serpentine. The 'slider' was placed thirty-two inches from the ground and was used for dressing. There are also designs for 'Corner bason stands' which varied from the very simple type of which many survive, consisting of four tiers, the lowest for a chamber pot, the second with a drawer for razors, etc., the third for the basin itself and its accompanying soap dishes, and the top with just room for a glass; and one designed so that it could be used 'in a genteel room without giving offence to the eye', and which was completely enclosed by doors and a tambour shutter above.

A sideboard illustrated in the Appendix to the *Drawing Book* has drawers to the front and sides, and a tambour shutter below the centre drawer, besides which end pedestals and knife boxes and an elaborate brass rail, with candle sconces. It is interesting that in some cases the sideboard was bow-fronted, and to keep to the correct proportions, this sometimes made the pieces extremely deep. Silver chamber pots from this period survive, which presumably were kept in the sideboard; some, however, had long handles and were passed under the table, for it was not permitted to leave the dining-room, at least in drinking clubs, until one was quite drunk. Generally, however, there was no great change in the design of sideboards during the last twenty years of the eighteenth century.

There is no doubt that furniture-making during the years 1775–1795 reached the highest degrees of skill and craftsmanship, but it lacked the robust vitality of the earlier years of the century. During the last years, in fact, a reaction set in against Adam neo-classicism, which is exemplified in the work of Henry Holland, who though influenced by Adam, soon moved

132 A Sheraton oval satinwood Pembroke table with an inlaid top and drawer fronts.

133 Sheraton's design for a summer bed in two compartments 'so that two people might sleep separately in hot weather'.

towards greater simplicity of elevation and plasterwork. This may be noted in his work at Brooks' Club, which opened in 1778, in which the rooms are simple and well proportioned, and in the alterations at Althorpe which he undertook from 1787. In 1784 he began work for the Prince of Wales at Carlton House Terrace, and in 1795 his most famous work at Southill, where he relies on simple plaster mouldings to form a background for furniture and pictures, rather than on bold decoration to dominate the

95

134 A Sheraton rosewood sofa-table with a plain stretcher, of about 1785.

scene. With Holland, Sir John Soane and John Nash also sought a simpler ideal.

Sheraton, in the *Cabinet Directory* of 1803, noted that marquetry furniture was out of fashion, and less inlaid work was done, more reliance being placed in the vivid colouring of the woods like maple and zebrawood. Curves began to replace straight lines; chair legs, which remained of light form during the first years of the nineteenth century, became thicker and the scimitar leg was introduced. Stools were made with X-framed supports or consisted of two supports in the shape of two C's placed back to back, often with lions' heads or leopards' heads. Brass inlay became popular, and for a short period during the first decade of the century, Egyptian motifs were adopted in tables, cabinets and chairs. There was an attempt to escape to a purer classicism, which is reflected in Sheraton's designs for a Greek table in his book of 1803; and there is a remarkable likeness between the later Sheraton designs, with their lions' heads, sphinxes and eagles, with their bold curves and scrolls, and the furniture produced by the Palladian architects of the 1720's.